"The most witty of all Oriental mystics translated   by the funniest of all American philosophers, who could ask for anything more? Lao Tse and Tim Leary fit together so well I almost believe in reincarnation."
—ROBERT ANTON WILSON

"As a luminous trajectory, starting from Tao wisdom   of the 6th Century BC and landing in the American scene as it enters the 21st Century, Psychedelic Prayers presents us with visions and choices we can no long ignore."
—LAURA HUXLEY

"Psychedelic Prayers is perhaps the best-loved among Leary's many books, and occupies a unique place in psychedelic literature."
—MICHAEL HOROWITZ

"Two of my 'oldest' friends: Lao Tse and Timothy, deep in conversation, speak with one voice."
—RAM DASS

✝ Timothy Leary

Psychedelic Prayers

& other meditations

INTRODUCTION
Ralph Metzner

BIBLIOGRAPHICAL PREFACE
Michael Horowitz

PREFACE
Rosemary Woodruff Leary

RONIN PUBLISHING, Inc.
Berkeley California

Psychedelic Prayers and Other Meditations

ISBN: 0-914171-84-4
ISBN: 978-0-914171-84-3
Copyright ©1997 by the Futique Trust

Published by
Ronin Publishing
P.O. Box 3436
Oakland CA 94609

www.roninpub.com
www.leary.com

Originally published as *Psychedelic Monograph II* by Poets Press
Library of Congress Catalog Card Number 66-23650
Copyright ©1966 by Timothy Leary

Project Editors:	Sebastian Orfali & Beverly Potter
Manuscript Editors:	Michael Horowitz, Ralph Metzner,
	Rosemary Woodruff Leary
Copy Editor:	Dan Joy
Cover Design:	Brian Groppe
Book Design:	Judy July
Production & Pre-Press:	Generic Type

Art, Illustrations, Photos: Page border from wood box edition which apprears on Dedication page, and as vignettes throughout this edition by Michael Green. Photos on pages 11, 12 & 126 by Peter Gould. Photo on page 30 by Robert Altman. Illustration on page 118 by Bill Ogden.

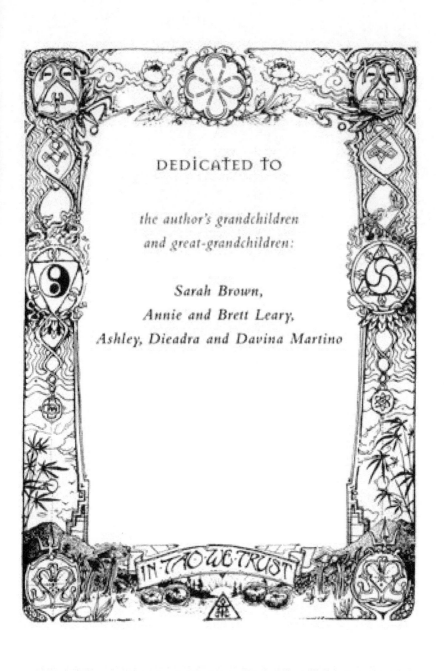

DEDICATED TO

*the author's grandchildren
and great-grandchildren:*

*Sarah Brown,
Annie and Brett Leary,
Ashley, Dieadra and Davina Martino*

IN TAO WE TRUST

TAO TE CHING

PSYCHEDELIC

PRAYERS

TABLE OF CONTENTS

Ralph Metzner with Nanette and Timothy Leary at the Taj Mahal, 1965.

introduction

RALPH METZNER

The first time I heard Tim Leary broach the idea of adapting the Tao Te Ching as a guide-book for psychedelic sessions was in Zihuatanejo, in the summer of 1962, during our first intensive retreat devoted to the exploration and mapping of the unusual states of consciousness opened up by psychedelics. We were working on the adaptation of the Tibetan Book of the Dead as a manual for psychedelic sessions that was later published as The Psychedelic Experience. In that text, Tim explained, the main teaching was to recognize the beautiful and horrible visions that one encountered, what the Bardo Thödol called the "peaceful and wrathful deities," as emanations or projections of one's own mind. With such recognition, triggered by the spoken words of the guide, one could avoid grasping for the beauties and fleeing from the terrors, stay centered and have a reasonable chance of making it through the experience to a balanced re-entry or "rebirth." Summing up the basic advice repeated many times throughout this guidebook, we would tell psychedelic voyagers to "relax and float down stream."

In one of our discussions Tim said that after we produced the Tibetan Book of the Dead manual, we would adapt the Tao Te Ching, which he considered a spiritually more advanced text. The book's essential teaching, for all of life, was to be like water . . . to keep flowing. This was my introduction to the teachings of Taoism, as the work on the Tibetan Book of the Dead was my introduction to Buddhism. Both have remained treasured parts of my life ever since. Neither my undergraduate education at Oxford nor the psychology graduate program at Harvard had included any exposure to Eastern philosophies or religion. So it was with a great deal of intellectual excitement that I started to delve into these texts, both of which are among the pre-eminent classics of the world's spiritual literature.

I believe my experience also paralleled that of Leary. A psychologist highly trained and skilled in the Western methods of scientific research, he felt affirmed in his spiritual approach to psychedelic experiences by the discovery of these ancient spiritual writings. Their essential message, once freed from the prevailing cultural symbolism, was fully consistent with the insights coming from psychedelic experiences. Psychedelic drugs and plants are catalysts for transcendent experiences—or they can be, given the appropriate preparation, attitude, and context (the "set and setting," in Leary's felicitous phrase).

The Asian spiritual texts are centrally concerned with transcendence, with learning to go beyond the ego-centered perspectives of ordinary human consciousness, beyond the dualities of right and wrong, and with becoming liberated from the fears and cravings that characterize human existence. For the traditional Asian religious teachers, the method of attaining such liberating transcendence was not psychedelics but meditation. Their goal, however, was essentially the same as that of spiritually oriented psychedelic explorers.

The period of the early sixties, when these explorations of consciousness and rediscoveries of ancient spiritual traditions were being made, was a time of extraordinary excitement and challenge for Leary, Alpert, myself, and the other psychologists of the Harvard project. Unimaginable potentials for human transformation were seemingly being opened up. Along with repeated experiences of transcendent states of consciousness through psychedelics, we were experiencing a transcendence of the usual framework of life in an academic institution. In 1962, Leary and Alpert were dismissed from Harvard, my graduate studies were completed, and the psychedelic research project that was initiated there had to find a new home. None of us were particularly disappointed or hurt by this apparent disgrace. As Tim was to say, it was as "unreasonable to expect a university to sponsor research in psychedelics as it would be to expect the Vatican to sponsor research in aphrodisiacs."

The research and explorations of consciousness continued unabated: at first with a training seminar in Zihuatanejo (which ended with our group being expelled from Mexico) and then (after unsuccessful attempts to continue the seminar in two Caribbean islands) in a magnificent mansion owned by the Hitchcock brothers in Millbrook, New York. In the late summer

PETER GOULD

**The Millbrook Big House in 1965,
at the time the Psychedelic
Prayers were written.**

of 1963, a group of about a dozen of us, including Tim and his two children Susan and Jack, Dick Alpert, my wife Susan and myself, and several others, convened in Millbrook and hunkered down for the fall and winter. Having been rebuffed in our attempts to establish a public psychedelic research center that would make these extraordinary new tools accessible to anyone with a responsible attitude, we decided to retreat and concentrate on writing and lecturing and our own personal work of transformation using psychedelics and meditation.

It was a time of great creative fervor for all of us, but especially for Leary. Many papers describing our work were written, lectures given, conference presentations made. The Psychedelic Experience was published in early 1964. I continued to edit and publish the Psychedelic Review, with the assistance of Paul Lee and Rolf von Eckartsberg. We started to give work-

Leary in
Millbrook, 1966,
with the psy-
chedelic dog,
Fang, and Diane
di Prima's
daughter,
Jeanne.

PETER GOULD

shops, in which altered states of consciousness and changes in perception
were induced without chemical means. We called ourselves the Castalia
Foundation, after the mystical retreat center in Hermann Hesse's novel The
Glass Bead Game.

Our experiences in Mexico and the Caribbean, as well as in earlier group
experiences when we were still at Harvard, had brought us right up against
some very heavy barriers to communication and cooperation—jealousy, pos-
sessiveness, competitiveness, envy, and so forth. There were also experiences of feeling a warm inclusive unity and non-possessive love for all beings.
However, after these experience wore off, the pre-imprinted feelings of the
normal personality returned, made perhaps more acutely uncomfortable by
the memory of the free consciousness experienced under the drug. The higher, more unified level of consciousness could not be maintained. We saw how
we were trapped by ancient patterns of conditioning.

Perhaps naively, we wanted to see if we could override them by consciously and intentionally choosing to do so. We began a series of small group experiments in non-possessive relationships, which were mostly abandoned after a couple of weeks as being too artificial. Out of all this, however, came some powerful learning and much laughter at the ridiculousness of our preconditioned attitudes and habits and the difficulty of escaping from them. Tim Leary's leadership style in these situations was light, humorous, and very engaging. Dick Alpert too had a great sense of humor and told fantastically intriguing stories of his adventures on the lecture circuit. The jazz musician Maynard Ferguson, together with his wife Flo and their three children, lived in the house as well. We all became very close.

When we were not working on writing, lecturing or giving workshops, or trying to free our interpersonal relationships from pre-imprinted possessive conditioning, we spent time working on the fantastic grounds of the three thousand acre estate, clearing shrubbery and building little retreat centers and hermit's nooks. I remember winter walks in the moonlight, when the only sound was the crunching of our boots in the snow. One crisp, cold day in November 1963 we got the synchronistic news: Aldous Huxley, the wise elder of the psychedelic movement, had died, and had taken a dose of LSD to facilitate the final journey; and on the same day, John F. Kennedy, our charismatic president, was assassinated in Dallas. This was a low body-blow to the collective American psyche—a sudden loss of innocence and idealism, and an ominous foreboding to those involved in the movement for the liberation of consciousness.

During the spring and summer of 1964 the Millbrook group continued their psychedelic explorations, creative writing projects, gardening, and connecting with artists, musicians, philosophers, researchers, journalists. Ken Kesey and his busload of Merry Pranksters arrived unannounced one day, after their legendary cross-country tour. Amazing feasts and celebrations took place in the extravagantly baroque mansion that we called the Big House. Millbrook became a kind of Mecca for psychedelic seekers and adventurers.

Among the constant stream of visitors from New York was a Swedish fashion model named Nanette, whose long-legged form was at that time adorning numerous New York transit buses. She and Tim fell in love and moved in together. Shortly thereafter, a friend of hers, another model named Kathy, with auburn hair and green eyes, arrived. Kathy and I fell in love. Both Tim and I, introverted intellectuals that we were, felt initially awkward with these glamorous and sophisticated denizens of the New York fashion world. Our LSD experiences with them however swiftly took us all to undreamed of levels of archetypal tantric spirituality.

Another Hermann Hesse novel that had made a deep impression on us was Journey to the East, a story of a group vision quest, a metaphorical journey to the lands of mystic spirituality. Each of the seekers on that journey had a personal goal, but all shared the goal of enlightenment and liberation. "For our goal," Hesse wrote, "was not only the East, or rather the East was not only a country and something geographical, but it was the home and youth of the soul." In Hesse's novel, the group quest, though initially ecstatically inspiring, falls apart under mysterious circumstances in a doomed place called Morbio Inferiore. We were also reading Ouspensky's In Search of the Miraculous and Gurdjieff's Meetings with Remarkable Men, in which a 20-year quest in Asia by a group called the Seekers after Truth is described. Stimulated by these accounts of spiritual quests, the idea of an actual geographical pilgrimage to India had formed in our minds.

So when the opportunity arose to accompany an Indian holy woman, Gayatri Devi, with her group of Indian and American disciples, on an ashram pilgrimage to India, I jumped at the chance and tried to persuade Kathy to go with me. Tim and Nanette wanted to join us some time later. Gayatri Devi, or Mataji as she was called, was a teacher in the lineage of Ramakrishna and Vivekananda, who had founded ashrams in Los Angeles and Boston, had tried LSD and was supportive of the exploration of its spiritual potentials. So in November of 1964 I found myself on the plane to India in her company. Kathy had become very anxious and conflicted and could not bring herself to go with me, though she held out hope she might come later. After a week's stopover in Kyoto, Japan, where we conversed with Zen teachers and visited shrines and temples, we landed in Calcutta, where

Mataji had thousands of devotees. Enormously interesting visits to temple sites in Bhubhaneshwar, Puri, Konarak and Benares followed. Then we went to Delhi and northwards up into the hill country of Uttar Pradesh to Rishikesh, where the Beatles later visited the ashram of Maharashi Mahesh Yogi.

Then I separated from Gayatri Devi's group and continued further northwards and into the Himalayan foothills to the village of Almora. Lama Anagarika Govinda, the Austrian-born Buddhist scholar, lived there with his Parsee wife, Li Gotami, in a cottage on a ridge with an unbelievably spectacular view of the snow and ice peaks of the Himalayas. Every day I would walk a couple of hours to their house and discuss various aspects of Tibetan Buddhist teachings with them. Lama Govinda was impressed with the appreciative dedication we had written to him in our adaptation of the Tibetan Book of the Dead. He agreed to try a dose of LSD that I offered to provide and guide for him. After an initially turbulent period of confusion and anxiety at the intense somatic changes induced, he centered himself with the aid of mantra and mudra, and had an illuminating experience according to the model of Bardo Thödol. He expressed his pleased anticipation of a visit from Timothy Leary.

During my travels in India I had been writing Kathy and the Millbrook group my impressions of India. Tim wrote back letters in which he described the fantastic and joyous spiritual and social carnival that Millbrook had become, his deepening relationship with Nanette, their wedding, their travel plans for India, and his evolving ideas about the processes of psychedelic consciousness expansion. He was using the ethological language of imprinting. These ideas and understandings formed the conceptual framework for his work in translating the Tao Te Ching into a session manual for psychedelic experiences. Here are a few excerpts from these letters:

The political-education battle over psychedelics has been won and from now on it's just a matter of time... next generation... my only concern now is to learn to use my own head and to pursue the incredible complexities that develop when two people begin to explore their poten-

tialities together and in small tribal groups. Withdrawing energy
and commitment from externals and materials, etc. You know.

Nanette and I have been together almost every minute
for the last three weeks and she is an unending series of
beauty and wise lessons... We are visiting the
Episcopalian minister in town to arrange the most roman-
tic, mythic wedding in history... very soon. You have to
give everything to it without reserve and then it all flows
from one moment of happiness to the next... well you
know. The tribal scene is wonderful.

The trees are now leafless and etched black, like
sumi-painting strokes, and the dusk comes quickly late
afternoons and fires are glowing in most of the rooms and
the house breathes softly waiting for the next period of
change and movement... Nanette and I will probably be
joining you after the first of the year.

The meaning of imprinting is "getting involuntarily
hooked to externals, accidentally presented externals at
that!!!" The process of de-imprinting is getting consciousness back to the flow and back to the body. Re-imprinting
is planned temporary hooking back to externals.

Marriage plans... we are inseparable these days, keeping humor and loving detachment while the turmoil swirls
by. We think now we'll leave for the Orient right after the
wedding.

My understanding of the "trap of externalization"
becomes clearer. Imprinting freezes us to the outside—the
trick is to withdraw once a week and then, each time, make
a carefully planned re-addiction to the outside—systemati-
cally reducing the number of externals—and thus allowing
for new complexity and subtlety. You know.

Nanette has changed. More quiet, tranquil, amazing
patience, she moves through the turmoil areas with calm. She
has Chinese, Viking, south Sweden farm girl things at her core.

The power of imprinting continually astounds me. Frightening, unless you continually and vigilantly recognize. We delight in the prospect of seeing you soon.

Richard (Alpert) has mutated. He has taken over "Tim's role," whatever that means, and is genial, hospitable, radiating plans and welcomes. He is filling the house with creative men and beautiful women...Wedding in four days. Incredibly long list of details all clicking into place. Nanette is a pure, white fire of honesty and love. We have been together about 23 hours a day for the last four weeks.

Kathy... every hour a new crisis. Nanette and I have bought her a ticket around the world which she now has in her possession. I have made reservations for her to leave when we leave. We are putting no pressure on her—simply giving her another card in her hands—a freedom card which she may or may not use. She is miserable. Your letters have been magnificent. I guess that is all you can do... let her know you are waiting, without putting on a lot of pressure or emotion. Perhaps by the time you receive this she will be on her way.

In any case, and in all cases the only thing to do is to free oneself from internal distortions and external addictions.

We think of you always and with great joy that we'll be with you soon.

I was deeply moved and exhilarated by Tim's letters. Readers of Psychedelic Prayers will recognize the themes of freeing oneself from "internal distortions and external addictions" in his versions of Lao Tse's ancient text. The Taoist teaching on the importance of attuning oneself with the flow of Tao resonates naturally with his statement that "de-imprinting is getting back to the flow and back to the body." As his letters show, he was acutely sensitive to the fragility and vulnerability of the imprinting process involved in human love relationships. There was an exquisite poignancy for me in his messages, since my romance with Kathy was hanging in the balance. For Tim and Nanette, although they could hardly have known this, their visit to the Himalayan village of Almora involved extraordinarily heightened creativity and spiritual insight, but it also spelled the beginning of the end of their marriage.

I took the three day journey by bus and train down from the Hill Country to meet Tim and Nanette in Delhi. When I told them enthusiastically about Almora and my meetings with Lama Govinda, they decided they wanted to go there too. But before we headed back up into the mountains, we wanted to see the Taj Mahal. We had heard that once a month, around the time of the full moon, the grounds are kept open to visitors at night. We thought this would be an extraordinary setting for a psychedelic experience. During the day we took a tour of the mausoleum, our senses heightened by legally available ganja. Our guide enthusiastically explained the history behind this amazing structure. "Shah Jehan, who built this monument, was not only in love with his wife, Mumtaz Mahal ('Jewel of the Palace') but he also had a mania for construction." He built it in response to his wife's dying request to create something by which she would be remembered.

Tim Leary was very impressed by the fact that Shah Jehan built the Taj as an expression of personal-human love. He felt that the quest for enlightenment still always had an element of selfishness ("my enlightenment") whereas the Shah's love for his wife was purely other-oriented. The question of how personal passionate human love could be integrated with the spiritual quest for liberation was clearly a central concern for Tim during this period—and perhaps a core theme of his entire post-psychedelic life.

As the sun was setting and the full moon rising, we set up our session blanket on the grass in front of the Taj. The sight of the Taj Mahal in the moonlight is indescribable, even with normal perception. After our eyes got adapted to the darkness, the light of the moon was brilliant as daylight, the white marble dome glistened pale blue and silver, while precious stones inlaid high on the dome flashed and sparkled. Like a mirage it hung in space, separated from the earth by a thin band of haze, glowing and humming with radiance in perfectly harmonious wave-field patterns.

In his autobiography Flashbacks Leary described how in Almora, they rented a house high on the ridge, with me in the guest room, and started a routine of visiting Lama Govinda and Li Gotami every afternoon. "It turned out that the Lama and I shared an intellectual obsession—a compulsive penchant for classification." Govinda had made an exhaustive study of Asian systems of consciousness and Leary, the author of Interpersonal Diagnosis of Personality, had spent years studying Western systems of personality. They got along famously.

Tim had brought along nine English language translations of the Tao Te Ching. Each day, sitting on the grass in the warm sun under the pine trees, he would pick one of Lao Tse's verses, read each of the versions and attempt to distill the essential meaning—using the perspectives gained from his psychedelic experiences. Lao Tse's cryptic and profound meditations on the invisible, all-pervasive universal energy flow process, were rendered into language that psychedelic voyagers would recognize from their experiences. Then he would reduce them down to the sparest possible formulations, distilling, extracting the essence, carving words like a sculptor hewing and polishing the stone to reveal the figure. Lao Tse had been a counselor to rulers and princes. Leary translated his advice to them into suggestions for the psychedelic session guide.

I feel these meditations on psychedelic consciousness expansion are perhaps Tim Leary's most inspired writings. They are, by turns, serene, sensuous, funny, and wise. He continued to work on them after he had returned to Millbrook, where they were organized as a session manual in six parts, to be read by the voyager or guide before and during a session. I suggested the name "Psychedelic Prayers." The six parts, corresponding roughly to the outline of The Psychedelic Experience, were (1) preparatory, (2) highest point of pure energy flow, (3) visions of biological or seed energy, (4) verses focusing on the perceptual senses, (5) verses focusing on the chakras, and (6) verses about re-entry, re-imprinting, or return to everyday life.

The three of us also visited Sri Krishna Prem, an expatriate Englishman who had lived in an ashram as devotee of Krishna-Radha in the nearby village of Mirtola for over forty years. He was an extraordinary figure, who had integrated Hindu and Buddhist teachings with the esoteric wisdom traditions of the West, including Gurdjieff. Where Govinda was a scholar, a pandit, Krishna Prem was truly a sage—a very down-to-earth, unassuming, humble and humorous one. After our initial visit, Tim went back once more by himself. I believe that with Krishna Prem Tim was probably the closest that he ever came to accepting a spiritual teacher. In Flashbacks he called Krishna Prem "The Wisest Man in India."

For me, the meeting with Sri Krishna Prem was also a turning point. When he talked about the so-called "left-hand path" of the siddhas, the tantric yogis of ancient times, he interpreted this to be the path of integrating the weaker, less developed function. I realized that my meetings and readings with Lama Govinda were only strengthening my intellect, which was already over-developed. I suddenly got the strong feeling that I should go back to the States so that I could piece together my fractured romance with the insecure Kathy. In addition, it was obvious that the relationship between Tim and Nanette was undergoing increasing strain, and I felt I should leave them alone to work things out. It was after all their honeymoon. What was I doing there? I left shortly thereafter.

When I returned to Millbrook, it was to a scene of depressing chaos. A seedy, drugged-out guy met me at the door wearing my clothes. Gone were the serenity and glowing warmth of Castalia weekends, the joyous enthusiasm for consciousness exploration in a family of seekers. Instead, the Millbrook mansion had become an Addams Family house of horrors, a scene of decadence and depravity and dabbling in black arts, of lost souls wandering around in permanently drugged states, of vicious conflicts leading at times to physical violence. Kathy's love for me had turned to hate, as she blamed my and Tim's absence for the destruction of the Millbrook dream. When Tim and Nanette, their relationship in tatters, returned to Millbrook some weeks later, he wrote of "the changes that had converted Millbrook from a community of scholars and scientists to a playground for rowdy omnisexuals." Millbrook had become our Morbio Inferiore.

The league of seekers did, however, recover from this debacle. Leary, Alpert and myself all went onto other phases of the story, told in other books, other high adventures in consciousness exploration. Nanette went on to marry an American Buddhist monk, who became an eminent scholar-teacher of Tibetan Buddhism; one of their daughters is a famous film

actress. A tantric love goddess arrived for Timothy in the form of the very beautiful Rosemary Woodruff. The Millbrook community flowered again with music, meditation, laughter, creativity, happy children, and remarkable people.

Leary's path after this took him increasingly into the role of pioneering social change activist. His fearless honesty and brilliant mockery in expressing radical viewpoints made him many enemies in high places. He had the dubious honor of being called "the most dangerous man in America" by none other than Richard Nixon. He spent upwards of 50 months in jail on several continents, an experience that left him without bitterness, but with razor-sharp insight into the American political system. He wrote 20 more books, developed theories and models of consciousness and contributed to numerous group creative projects. He married two more times and became a great-grandfather before his death in May, 1996. To hundreds of thousands of his friends and admirers, he remains one of the outstanding visionary geniuses of the 20th century. To me he was the perfect exemplar of one of those who in the last of the Psychedelic Prayers are listed as likely to be closer to the Tao—"smiling men with bad reputations."

I don't believe he ever again had the opportunity to devote himself so completely to the exploration and description of spiritual development, and how higher states of consciousness can be integrated into ongoing life. His psychedelic prayers based on the Tao Te Ching integrate ancient Eastern wisdom teachings with the insights of modern science, and the practical knowledge gained from direct experience of expanded states of consciousness. They provide the spiritual seeker using psychedelics with an unsurpassed guidebook to the realization of the highest potentials of the human mind and of these amazing substances.

Ralph Metzner
Sonoma, California
October, 1996

PSYCHEDELIC
PRAYER BOOK

Timothy Leary
and
Ralph Metzner
with added commentary
by
Rabbi Zalman Schachter

First Edition
Castalia Foundation
Millbrook, N Y
1966

**Hand-drawn title-page of the
pre-publication version.**

BIBLIOGRAPHICAL PREFACE

The Publishing History of **Psychedelic Prayers**
with a Note on the Text of This Edition

MICHAEL HOROWITZ

W ritten while Timothy Leary was visiting India in 1965 and finished at his celebrated commune-estate in Millbrook, New York the following year, *Psychedelic Prayers* is a series of 55 poems divided in six sections, adapted from the 37 chapters of Book I of *Tao Te Ching (Way of Life)*, composed by the immortal Chinese Taoist philosopher and keeper of the Royal Archives, Lao Tse, in the 6th century B.C.

Leary was drawn to the "psychedelic" quality of the ancient work. "My objective," he later wrote, "was to find this seed idea in each sutra and rewrite it in the *lingua franca* of psychedelia." Leary succeeded brilliantly in his aim: intended for guided meditational use during LSD sessions, *Psychedelic Prayers* is perhaps the best-loved among his many books, and occupies a unique place in psychedelic literature.

Psychedelic Prayers has an interesting publishing history. The first edition was printed by famed Beat poet Diane di Prima at her Poets Press in Kerhonkson, NY, not far from Millbrook. The first edition was printed on textured paper and bound in pink wrappers; between one and two thousand copies were printed. The second edition was printed on laid paper in five different colored inks for psychedelic effect, and bound in yellow wrappers; two to three thousand copies of this edition were published (but not printed) by the Poets Press.

Psychedelic artist Michael Bowen created a Hindu design for the front wrapper of both editions; the back wrapper bears the publisher's alchemical emblem. The author dedicated his book to William and Aurora Hitchcock, his Millbrook benefactors. Both editions appeared in the spring of 1966, about a year before the psychedelic zeitgeist reached its zenith.

University Books of New Hyde Park, NY, publishers of *The Psychedelic Experience* (1964), brought out the third edition in August 1966: a photo-offset copy of the first edition, printed in dark brown ink, with nearly identical wrappers to the second edition, in a print run of 5,000 copies.

The fourth edition appeared in the early 1970s under the imprint of the League for Spiritual Discovery, a religious organization founded by Leary in 1967 and based upon the sacramental use of psychedelic substances. Once again the text was printed by photo-offset; the front and back covers have entirely different designs by Dion Wright. This edition, published by the Mystic Arts Bookshop in Laguna Beach, is dedicated to The Brotherhood of Eternal Love, the legendary group of underground LSD distributors of the brand named Sunshine. This edition appeared after the author escaped prison and fled with his wife Rosemary to North Africa and Europe. The printing was very small, probably no more than 2,000 copies, and intended to raise money for the legal expenses of the fugitive Learys.

The fifth North American edition is the most rare and unique. Only 100 sets were printed in purple ink, with each poem on a separate leaf having a border design depicting sacred plants executed by Michael Green. The calligraphy was done by Daniel Raphael. Each set of sheets was contained within a customized wooden box with a sliding top panel on which the title was carved. The work was produced in Montreal in 1972 through the efforts of Rosemary Leary, then separated from her husband and living underground as a fugitive. It was not intended for commercial sale; each leaf was supposed to represent "script" (i.e., currency) which could be traded like a share of stock.

The text of the *Prayers* varies greatly in this edition: 49 (of the 55 total poems) were printed, one to a page (necessitating some cuts in the longer poems) with a number stamped on the verso of each sheet. The arrangement of many of the poems on the page differs from their original lay-out, with aesthetic considerations uppermost. Leary expressed satisfaction with this edition—particularly the notion of poetry as "script," for the author and his wife had sometimes resorted to producing impromptu manuscripts which they sold for money in order to survive in exile.

The first British edition, published by Academy Editions, London, also appeared in 1972. This edition follows the text of the first edition, and is enhanced with Chinese landscape drawings.

The first foreign translation, a bilingual edition printed in German and English, appeared in Bern, Switzerland from the publisher Mantram in 1975 with a dust jacket designed by Swiss artist Hans Giger, later of *Alien* fame. Two other friends of the exiled Learys, the British writer Brian Barritt, and Swiss author Sergius Golowin, wrote introductions. Pirated editions of the German translation appeared from God's Press in Amsterdam & Kathmandu in 1975, and from Volksverlag in Linden, Germany in 1982.

A possibly unique, self-described "pre-publication manuscript" (actually, mimeographed) copy in the Ludlow Library bears the variant title *Psychedelic Prayer Book*. (This copy belonged to Rt. Rev. Michael Francis Itkin, known in New York's East Village during the mid-1960s as the "psychedelic priest.") The author's Harvard and Millbrook colleague Ralph Metzner is listed as co-author, and Rabbi Zalman Schachter (whose LSD trip with Leary at Millbrook is documented in *High Priest*) provided some "added commentary." In their one-page introduction, Leary and Metzner describe this edition as "being given to a few friends" with the "hope you will send us your ideas for improving" the work.

Advertisement for *Psychedelic Prayers* from *East Village Other.*

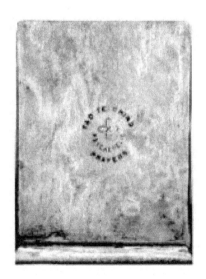

Poets Press edition

University Books edition

Wood Box edition

League for Spiritual
Discovery edition

First U.K. edition

First German edition:
dust jacket art by H.R. Giger

A NOTE ON THE TEXT OF THIS EDITION

T wo poems from Part V (V-7 and V-8) have been moved to Part II (where they are now II-8 and II-9) as it seemed to the editors these poems properly belonged to an earlier stage of the psychedelic experience.
Six new poems from later chapters of the *Tao Te Ching* were adapted by the author and his wife Rosemary in Laguna Beach, California about two years after the first publication of the book, and published in the January 17, 1969 issue of New York City's underground newspaper the *East Village Other* under the title "Poems on the Conduct of Life." The text of the poems is preceded by a 600-word preface in which the author discusses, at times from new perspectives, the importance of the *Tao Te Ching,* and states his intention of publishing "a new Taoist guidebook which could be called How To Live The Turned-On Life In An Uptight Society." Five of the poems are reprinted here in newly edited versions (the sixth poem is an experimental sound poem that is better recited than printed).

A final poem has been added at the end of the present edition. "Homage to the Awe-full Seer," the longest poem in the book, was originally published in *Psychedelic Review* no. 9 in 1967. Although not a translation from the *Tao te Ching,* the theme of the poem closely associates it with the wisdom-message of the ancient Chinese text and the impact made by the sage who wrote it.

Regarding the text of this edition, readers familiar with the original 1966 edition will notice occasional revision. The editors, who have all worked closely with Timothy Leary on literary projects, have been long aware of Leary's penchant for revising—often substantially—each of his books at the time of their re-publication. During the last months of his life Timothy knew of the plan to republish *Psychedelic Prayers*—which pleased him greatly—but was too ill to work on the new edition. He made it clear that he expected us to make changes we deemed necessary ("It's your call," he liked to say).

Ralph Metzner, co-author with Leary and Richard Alpert of *The Psychedelic Experience* (1964), assisted Leary when he first produced these translations in India in 1965, and as noted earlier is listed as co-author in the pre-publication, mimeographed edition of *Psychedelic Prayers.*

Rosemary Leary, who became engaged to the author while he was still completing work on this book, recited the prayers with her husband at public events during the mid-1960s, making revisions in the text as they went along; she worked on the adaptations of the additional poems published in 1969, and was responsible for the remarkable 1972 wooden box edition.

Michael Horowitz, the author's archivist and bibliographer, has performed editorial work on Leary's books for 25 years, from *Jail Notes* (1970) to *Chaos and Cyberculture* (1994).

While the editors had the author's encouragement and blessing in taking on the daunting task of re-editing this sacred text of psychedelic literature, they take full responsibility for any and all revisions, as Timothy Leary passed away (May 31, 1996) shortly before we began working on this new edition.

Note: The source for the bibliographical data in this article is: An Annotated Bibliography of Timothy Leary *by Michael Horowitz, Karen Walls, and Billy Smith (Archon Books, 1988). Acknowledgement is also made to The Fitz Hugh Ludlow Memorial Library, where the printed works herein described and illustrated were made available for examination.*

Rosemary and Timothy at their home in
Berkeley in 1968.

PREFACE

ROSEMARY WOODRUFF LEARY

In August 1965, a few months after we first met, Tim picked me up at my apartment in Manhattan and took me to the Millbrook Estate for a week or so before I left for California.

Tim led me to the tower room. The window overlooking the vast grounds was framed by a Hoya plant whose blossoms scented the air. Later that evening he brought a bottle of wine and a tattered manuscript to read by candlelight. His voice caressed me softly.

Gate of the Soft Mystery
Gate of the Dark Woman

I stayed awake all that night puzzling over his adaptations of Lao Tse. I didn't go to California.

Recently, I rediscovered a manuscript titled 108 Memories of Our Present Incarnation which Tim wrote for me while in the California State Prison at San Luis Obispo in 1970. In this passage Tim recalls writing one of the poems in Psychedelic Prayers:

"Number 17. Millbrook—During LSD session. We went upstairs and made love. I wrote the sex chakra poem in memory of your trembling earth beauty. Nov. '66"

A later reference in the same manuscript refers to reading the poems together on-stage during the road tour of the Psychedelic Celebrations later that winter:

"Number 42. Standing on stage at celebration reciting our poetry and hearing your soft voice echoing back. What beauty our love created for the world."

I'd like to think so.

The next few years brought summers of love and seminars, fall lecture tours, winter harassments, arrests and trials that culminated with Tim's prison escape and our flight to exile in Algeria and Switzerland. In the winter of 1972, after Tim and I had gone our separate ways, the *Psychedelic Prayers* re-entered my life. A fugitive, I was hiding out in a farmhouse near Ste. Agathe in Quebec. The snow reached above the first floor and the electricity was out. Again, by candlelight, I reread and edited the poems while my friend Brigitte collated the pages and baked oatmeal cookies and her husband Sergai made the beautiful boxes to contain them. We never made any money from this loving endeavor, but Brigitte and Sergai Mars, with their baby daughter Sunflower, traded them for food in health stores across the country. Brigitte later gave these sets to Dr. Oscar Janiger, Terence McKenna, and distinguished herbalists. Brigitte is including a few of the poems in her new book on herbs.

If you knew how to listen,
the seed would hum you a seed song.

It has been an immense pleasure to once again read and edit Tim's work, this time in the company of dear friends Ralph Metzner and Michael and Cindy Horowitz.

I hope that lovers and seekers finding these poems will

Keep in touch
and be at home
everywhere.

Rosemary Woodruff Leary
1996

Beloved -

Here are forty-nine sutras based on Book I of the
Tao Te Ching.

This pre-publication manuscript is being given to a few
friends. We hope they will enlighten you. We hope you will send
us your ideas for improving them.

The sutras are divided into five sections. For use in a
psychedelic session it is best to select two or three from each
section. They should be read very slowly and in a serene voice.
They should be considered prayers to be whispered.

Part I is read before the session. The sutra about the
guide is especially important since it sets up the contract for
conducting the session.

Part II contains sutras about pure energy. These prayers
are to be read at the highest point in a session.

Part III concerns biological or seed energy and can be
read during the very "high" points of the session.

Part IV is prepared for experiments in body awareness-
breaking through to chakras or somatic nerve centers.

Part V is to be read towards the end of the session- between
the eighth and twenty-fourth hour.

Keep in touch....

T.L.
R.M.

Early version of Introduction.

Timothy Leary on the cover of the *San Francisco Oracle* **(December 16, 1966).**

FOREWORD

TIMOTHY LEARY

The psychedelic or visionary experience releases a wide range of awareness-of-energy and tunes us in to patterns of neurological signals which are usually censored from mental life.

Understanding, description, and intelligent use of these released energies have puzzled scholars for thousands of years. Today, LSD sessions puzzle, enrapture, awe, and confuse.

Mainly they confuse.

During the last five years, 1960-65, we have witnessed a psychedelic revolution. Consider the statistics.

Over one hundred and fifty million Americans share the same imprinted symbol system—tribal language and rituals.

Of these, a good ten million have taken the first psychedelic step and experienced the neural level of consciousness—have transcended symbols and contacted raw energy hitting their nerve endings. Here we include the marijuana smokers, the adepts in hatha yoga, and meditators.

Another group, at least 500,000 Americans, have contacted cellular consciousness—have had experiences which transcend both symbolic game and the sensory apparatus. We include here the peyote eaters, the mushroom eaters, the LSD cult. If we add those millions of persons who have had an involuntary psychedelic experience, those institutionalized mystics we call psychotic, the ranks of this group swell to astounding proportions. More than any other group, psychotics need the sort of training and guidance provided by psychedelic manuals. They are whirled into realms of raw sensory bombardment and cellular hallucination—unprepared and socially anathematized. If psychotics were trained in the use of psychedelic manuals such as this volume they would have some understanding and control of the multi-level, multiple-exposure experiences we call hallucinatory.

Next we have those whose consciousness has gone beyond game, gone beyond direct sensory awareness, gone beyond cellular flow and contacted the molecular and elemental energies that crackle and vibrate within the cellular structure. Those who have taken large doses of LSD, mescaline, DMT, and experienced what the eastern psychologists call the "white light," the "void," the "inner light."

Each of these psychedelic levels—neural, cellular, molecular—are beyond symbols, incoherent to the symbolic mind. And each of these levels of consciousness is different from the others. This wide spectrum of whirling energies—all uncharted and unlabelled—confronts the psychedelic explorer.

So what is the net effect of these millions of visionary voyages?

A linguistic babel.

A chaos of potentiality.

A confusion of promise.

Most of these psychedelic voyagers are now aware of the limitless realities stored in the nervous systems, but there is no conception of the meaning and use of these potentials.

There are of course no pat solutions, no easy answers provided by LSD. On the contrary, every paradox, every ambiguity, every problem of static-symbolic life is intensified, raised to exponential powers. Where there once was a blind robot symbolic uncertainty (Johnson or Goldwater?), there is now an uncertainty compounded and multiplied by the knowledge of the illusory nature of routine reality and the existence of countless realities.

From the beginning of the Harvard-IFIF-Castalia exploration into consciousness two facts were apparent. First, that there were no extant maps, models, myths, theories, languages to describe the psychedelic experience. Second, that the temptation to impose old models, premature theories must be resisted.

No current philosophic or scientific theory was broad enough to handle the potential of the 13 billion-cell computer.

Our decision then was to maintain an open posture, to collect data on psychedelic sessions from a wide variety of subjects, in a wide variety of settings, and to continue to look for better models and theories to explain the psychedelic experience.

It became apparent that, in order to run exploratory sessions, manuals and programs were necessary to guide subjects through transcendental experiences with a minimum of fear and confusion. Rather than start de novo using our own minds and limited experiences to map out the voyage, we turned to the only available psychological texts which dealt with consciousness and its alterations—the ancient books of the East.

The Tibetan Book of the Dead is a psychedelic manual—incredibly specific about the sequence and nature of experiences encountered in the ecstatic state. A revision of this text published under the title The Psychedelic Experience was our first attempt at session programming.

For the last two years we have been working with another old, time-tested psychedelic manual—the Chinese text Tao Te Ching, sometimes translated as The Way of Life.

Written some 2600 years ago by one or several philosophers known to us now as "the old fellow" (Lao Tse), this text is still timelessly modern and will remain so for thousands of years to come—as long as man has the same sort of nervous system and deals with the range of energies he now encounters.

The Tao Te Ching deals with energy. Tao is best translated as "energy," as energy process. Energy in its pure unstructured state (the E of Einstein's equation) and energy in its countless, temporary states of structure (the M of Einstein's equation).

The Tao is an ode to nuclear physics, to life, to the genetic code, to that form of transient energy structure we call "man," to those most static, lifeless forms of energy we call man's artifacts and symbols.

The message of the Tao Te Ching is that all is energy, all energy flows, all things are continually transforming.

The Tao Te Ching is a series of 81 verses which celebrate the flow of energy, its manifestation and, on the practical side, the implications of this philosophy for man's endeavors. Most of the pragmatic sutras of the Tao were directed towards the ruler of a state. How can the king and his ministers use this knowledge of the energy powers to govern harmoniously?

Like all great biblical texts, the Tao has been rewritten and re-interpreted in every century and this is as it should be. The terms for Tao change in each century. In our times Einstein rephrases it, quantum theory revises it, the geneticists translate it in terms of DNA and RNA, but the message is the same.

The practical aspects of the Tao must also be rewritten and adapted to the everyday situation. The advice given by the smiling philosophers of China to their emperor can be applied to how to run your home, your office, and how to conduct a psychedelic session. The Tao Te Ching is divided into two books—the first comprising thirty-seven chapters, the second forty-four.

In this volume of Psychedelic Prayers from the Tao Te Ching you will find fifty-six poems which are based on the thirty-seven chapters of Book I of the original.

These translations from English to psychedelese were made while sitting under a bamboo tree on a grassy slope of the Kumaon Hills over-looking the snow peaks of the Himalayas.

The work went like this. I had nine English translation of the Tao. I would select a Tao chapter and read and reread all nine English versions of it. Each translator, of course, made his own interpretation of the flowing calligraphy. Nine western minds. But after hours of rereading and meditation the essence of the poem would slowly bubble up. The aim was to relate this essence theme to psychedelic sessions. Slowly a psychedelic version of the chapter would emerge.

The first draft version would then be put under the psychedelic microscope. For several years I have pursued the yoga of one LSD session every seven days. The neurological amplification of cannabis was also available. Each time our Moslem cook walked down to the village he would bring back a crayon-size stick of attar. Attar means essence. The essence resin of the marijuana plant is sometimes called hashish.

LSD opened up the lenses of cellular and molecular consciousness. Attar cleansed the windows of the senses.

During these sessions I would read the most recent draft of the Tao poems. A humbling experience for the poet—to have his words exposed to the pitiless magnification of the psychedelic perspective.

Psychedelic poetry, like all psychedelic art, is crucially concerned with flow. Each psychedelic poem is carefully tailored for a certain time in the sequence of the session. Simplicity and diamond purity are important. Intellectual flourishes and verbal pyrotechnics are painfully obvious to the "turned on" nervous system.

During these examinations a ruthless process of polishing, cutting away takes place. Slowly the most blatant redundancies and mentalisms were pruned.

Each poem in this volume has been exposed to several dozen appraisals by lysergicized nervous systems. Each psychedelic "try-out" is different. People's reactions vary. What is essence-simplicity to one, is truism to another. The "right" metaphor for one is contrived to another.

Most readers have found five or so poems in this collection which vibrate in tune to their deepest resonances. The rest do not pass the inspection of their psychedelic enlargers.

The fifty-six hymns have been divided into six groups:

Part I. Preparatory prayers to be read before the session. These hymns apply the creative quietude of Lao Tse to the technique of running a psychedelic session.

Part II. Prayers invoking pure energy flow, molecular or atomic energy beyond symbol, sense-organ or cellular energy. These prayers are to be read slowly and ethereally during the "high" points which usually come during the first three hours of an LSD session.

Part III. Prayers invoking cellular consciousness, seed energy. Odes glorifying the DNA code to be read from the third to sixth hour of the LSD session.

Part IV. Prayers invoking sensory experiences registered by the external sense organs. Hymns glorifying the direct awareness of vision, hearing, touch, smell, taste to be read from the sixth to ninth hours of the LSD session or during sessions involving neural ecstatagenic agents such as marijuana, low doses of LSD, hatha yoga, meditation.

Part V. Prayers invoking sensory experiences registered by internal sense organs, visceral awareness from the nerve plexes mediating elimination, sex, heart, lungs, and the frontal cortex. These hymns can be read during the sixth to ninth hours of an LSD session when the subject has cut himself off from external stimulation.

Part VI. *Re-imprinting prayers designed to guide the subject during the period of re-entry (nine to 24 hours), while the subject is returning to the symbolic world and the post-session imprint is being formed.*

These divisions are based on the theory of levels of consciousness developed during six years of psychedelic research and included in Static and Ecstatic Consciousness [this book remains unpublished–editor].

This mapping of consciousness is based on the neurological and biochemical anatomy of the human body.

The theory is simple.

Consciousness is energy received by structure.

There are as many dimensions of consciousness as there are structures in the body to receive and decode energy.

Any high school text in biology can be used to define the dimensions of consciousness.

1. There is the symbolic mind—that fraction of the nervous system which perceives, discriminates, interprets, remembers learned (i.e., conditioned) cues selectively imposed on the kaleidoscope of sensation. This is the imprinted mind. The prayers in Part VI of this volume are to be used during the latter stages of the psychedelic experience when the re-imprinting process begins to impose stasis on the ecstatic flow.

2. The nervous system defines the level of neural consciousness—direct, symbol-free registration of energies by nerve endings. The prayers in Part IV of this volume are hymns to the five exterior senses. Odes of gratitude and reverent readiness to attend to the tattoo of energies hitting the visual, auditory, tactile, olfactory and gustatory sense bulbs.

3. Interoceptive sensations are messages from internal organs. Most of these sensations are excluded from symbolic consciousness. Tibetan Buddhists and Tantric Hindus have worked for centuries with methods of contacting interior sensations and maps for symbolizing them. These levels of internal consciousness are

*called chakras. Part V of this volume includes hymns to five class-
es of internal sensations—messages from the eliminative, sexual,
cardiac, respiratory and fore-brain centers.*

*4. The unit of life, the building block of the tissues and organs
mediated by the nervous system, is the cell. The cell is a highly
complicated structure for registering and transforming energy.
Every cell in your body is an organization network more complicated than the city of New York. The cell registers and decodes
energy and remembers. The cell is in communicative contact with
the grosser level of consciousness of the nervous system. The
brain of the cell is DNA. The afferent-efferent nervous system of
the cell is RNA. Part III of this volume is made up of hymns prais-
ing the power and ancient wisdom of the cell, the seed consciousness of DNA.*

*5. Cells are composed of smaller structures—amino acid mole-
cules and atomic elements. These structures receive and decode
energy. They are older, wiser, more powerful than cells. The atom
uses molecules and cells the way the DNA code uses tissues,
organs and nervous systems and the way the symbolic mind uses
cars and tractors. Part II of this volume praises the wisdom of
molecular and atomic process, prepares you for this awesome
level of consciousness and guides you through it.*

*6. Part I of this volume collects those Tao prayers which are rele-
vant to guiding a psychedelic session. These prayers are not specific to any particular level of consciousness. They present the philosophy of creative quietude passed on by Lao Tse.*

The Tao manual, like all other psychedelic texts, must be studied
intensively, the detailed theory of energy transformations thoroughly
learned, and the commentary notes for those prayers selected for the
session reread several times.

Psychedelic poetry should be read aloud (or taped) at a slow tempo, in a low natural voice. The prayers are best read or taped by one who is "high" at the time. Any tension, artificiality or game-playing on the part of the reader stands out in embarrassing relief.

Read by the static intellect imprinted to symbols, and inundated by the verbosity of our culture, these sutras are simply another sequence of lifeless words. But to the consciousness released from imprinted statics these prayers can become precise bursts of trembling energy and breathless meaning.

You will wonder, perhaps, at the use of the term "prayer" to label these sutras.

Prayer is ecstatic poetry. Psychedelic communication.

Ordinary, static communication in terms of prose symbols, is game. Mind addressing mind.

You cannot describe the ecstatic moment in static terms.

You cannot (without regret) communicate during the ecstatic moment in static prose.

You cannot produce ecstasy with static symbol sequences.

When you are in a psychedelic state—out beyond symbols—game communication seems pointless. Irrelevant. Inappropriate. Inadequate.

There is no need to communicate—because everything is already in communication. You are plugged into the multiplex network of energy exchanges.

But there are those transition moments of terror, of isolation, of reverence, of gratitude...when there comes that need to communicate.

The need to communicate with the non-game energy source that you sense in yourself and around you.

And there is the need, at exactly that moment, for a language which is not mental or cliche. A straight, pure, "right" non-game language.

This is prayer — a Mantra — an Ejaculation.

There are moments in every psychedelic session when there comes that need to communicate—at the highest and best level you are capable of.

This need has been known and sensed for thousands of years. All prayers are originally psychedelic communications with higher freer energies—tuning yourself in to the billion-year-old energy dance.

Conventional prayers, for the most part, have degenerated into game rituals. Slogans. Meaningless verbalizations. Appeals for game help.

But that crucial non-game terror-reverence awe-full moment comes...

There comes that time when the ecstatic cry is called for.

At that time, you must be ready to pray.

To go beyond yourself. To contact energy beyond your game.

At that time you must be ready to pray.

When you have lost the need to pray...

You are a dead man in a world of dead symbols.

Pray for life.

Pray for life.

Timothy Leary
Kumaon Hills, Almora, India, 1965
Millbrook, New York, 1966

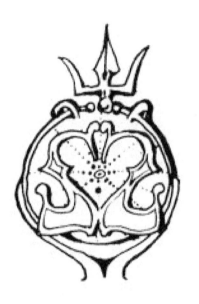

PART I

PRAYERS FOR PREPARATION

HOMAGE TO LAO TSE

I - 1

THE GUIDE

In the greatest sessions
One does not know that there is a guide

In the next best sessions
One praises the guide

It is worse when
One fears the guide
Or when one pays him

If the guide lacks trust in the people
The trust of the people will be lacking

The wise guide guards his words
And sits serenely

When the greatest session is over
The people will say:
"It all happened naturally"
"It was so simple, we did it all ourselves."

I - 2

When The Harmony Is Lost

When the harmony is lost
  Then come clever discussions and
"Wise men" appear

When the unity is lost
Then come "friends"

When the session is plunged
Into disorder
Then there are "doctors"

I - 3

LIFE, LIGHT, LOVE
SEED, SUN, SON
DEATH, DAUGHTER, DNA

Hold in reverence
This Great Symbol of Transformation
And the whole world comes to you

Comes to you without harm
Dwells in common wealth
Dwells in the union of Heaven and Earth

Offer music . . . food . . . wine . . .
And the passing guest will stay a while

But the molecular message
In its passage through the mouth
Is without flavor

It cannot be seen
It cannot be heard
It cannot be exhausted by use

It remains

I - 4

LET THERE BE SIMPLE NATURAL THINGS DURING THE SESSION

Let there be simple, natural things
to contact during the session–

hand woven cloth
uncarved wood
ancient music
flowers–growing things
burning fire
a touch of earth
a splash of water
fruit . . . good bread . . . cheese
wine
sacred smoke
candles
temple incense
a warm hand
anything more than five hundred years old

Of course it is always best to be
Secluded with nature

I - 5

All Things Pass

All things pass
   A sunrise does not last all morning
All things pass
  A cloudburst does not last all day
All things pass
  Nor a sunset all night

But Earth . . . sky . . . thunder . . .
  wind . . . fire . . . lake . . .
  mountain . . . water . . .
These always change

And if these do not last
Do man's visions last?
Do man's illusions?

During the session
Take things as they come

All things pass

I - 6

The Message Of Posture

During the session
Observe your body
Mandala of the universe

Observe your body
Of ancient design
Holy temple of consciousness
Central stage of the oldest drama

Observe its structured wonders
  Skin . . . hair . . . tissue
  Bone . . . vein . . . muscle
  Net of nerve

Observe its message
Does it merge or does it strain?
Does it rest serene on sacred ground
Or tilt, propped up by wire and sticks?

On tiptoe one cannot stand for long
Tension retards the flow

Superfluous noise and redundant action
Stand out–square, proud, cramped
Against the harmony

Observe the mandala of your body

PART II

THE EXPERIENCE OF ELEMENTAL ENERGY

HOMAGE TO THE ATOM

II - 1

That Which Is Called The Tao Is Not The Tao

The flow of energy . . .
Here . . . It . . . Is . . .

Nameless
Timeless
Speed of light

Float . . . beyond fear . . .
Float . . . beyond desire . . .
Into this Mystery of Mysteries
Through this Gate of All Wonder

II - 2

Ethereal Pool
Without Source

E mpty bowl of radiance
Full of starry universe
Silent void
Shimmering
Ancestor of all things

Here
All sharpness rounded
All wheels glide along
Soft tracks of light

Ethereal pool without source

Preface to life

II - 3

JEWELLED INDIFFERENCE

Galactic play
Belted radiance
Lethal spectrum
Restless diamond eye

Solar
So long
So long?

Jewelled indifference
   Where's home?
Jewelled indifference
   Where am I?
Jewelled indifference
   I want to go back!
Jewelled indifference
   Help! I don't understand!
Jewelled indifference
   Is it all a dream?

WARNING!
SOLAR SHUTTERS OPENING
LETHAL LOVE RADIATION BEWARE
FATAL UNITY BLISS FUSION

All right. Who's next?
"The sound man faces the passing of human
          generations
  immune as to a sacrifice of straw dogs"

Good bye now
Glide into fusion
Relentless diamond eye

There
We
Go

Good
Bye

II - 4

FALLING FREE

L aw of gravity . . . falling free
Falling free . . . the root of lightness

Repose . . . the seed of movement

Stillness . . . the master of agitation

Gravity . . . falling free

II - 5

Sheathing The Self

The play of energy endures
Beyond striving

The play of energy endures
Beyond body

The play of energy endures
Beyond life

Out here
Float timeless
Beyond striving

II - 6

Manifestation Of
The Mystery

Gazing, we do no see it
We call it empty space

Listening, we do not hear it
We call it silence

Reaching, we do not grasp it
We call it intangible

But here . . . we spin through it
Electric, silent, subtle

II - 7

PLEASE DO NOT CLUTCH AT THE GOSSAMER WEB

All in Heaven
On Earth below
A crystal fabric
Sacred gossamer web

Grabbing hands shatter it

Watch closely this shimmering mosaic

Silent . . .
Glide in
Harmony

II - 8

HOLD FAST TO THE VOID

Πotice how this space
Between Heaven and Earth
Is like a bellows

Always full, always empty

Come in here, go out there

Breathing . . .
Silence

This is no time for talk
Better to hold fast to the void

II - 9

Ŧᴀᴋᴇ İɴ–Lᴇŧ Gᴏ

Ŧo breathe in
You must first breathe out
Let go

To hold
You must first open your hand
Let go

To be warm
You must first be naked
Let go

PART III

THE EXPERIENCE OF SEED-CELL ENERGY

HOMAGE TO DNA

III - 1

THE SERPENT COIL OF DNA

We meet it everywhere
But do not see its front

We follow it everywhere
But do not see its back

When we embrace this ancient serpent coil
We are masters of the moment
And feel no break in the curling
Back to primeval beginnings

This may be called
Unravelling the clue of the life process

III - 2

Prehistoric Origins
Of DПA

I ts rising is not bright
Nor its setting dark

Unceasing, continuous
Branching out in roots innumerable
Forever sending forth the serpent coil
Of living things
Mysterious as the formless existence
To which it returns

Coiling back
Beyond mind

We say only it is
Formed from the formless
Life from spiral void

III - 3

CLEAR WATER

The seed of mystery
Lies in muddy water

How can we fathom this muddiness?
Water becomes clear through stillness

How can we become still?
By moving with the stream

III - 4

RETURNING TO THE SOURCE–REPOSE

B e empty
Watch quietly while the ten thousand forms
Swim into life and return to the source

Do nothing
Return to the source

Deep repose is the sign
That you have reached the appointed goal

To return to the source is to discover
The eternal law of seed

He who returns to this eternal law is enlightened
Being enlightened he is serene
Serene he is open-hearted
Open-hearted he is beyond social games
Being beyond social games he is in tune with seed
In tune with seed he endures

Until the end of his life he is not in peril

III - 5

Lao Tse's Mind Becomes Pre-occupied With A Very Difficult Subject:

To Describe The Production of Material Forms By The Tao

Is it a dream?
   Shadowy
   Elusive
   Invisible

All things, all images move slowly
Within shimmering nets

Here essence endures
From here all forms emerge
Back from this moment
To the ancient beginning

III - 6

Transfiguration Exercises

What was inert . . . moves
What was dead . . . . lives
What was drab . . . radiates

Galactic time has labored to produce
This moment
Exquisite

The ancient saying that the isolated part
Becomes whole
Was spoken wisely

Seed flows
All forms glow

Remain quiet . . .
Pulsate
In harmony

III - 7

THE TREE ABOVE—
THE TREE BELOW

W hat is above is below
What is without is within
What is to come is in the past

Tall . . . deep . . . tree . . . green . . . branching . . . leaf
Root . . . above . . . below . . . thrusting . . . coiling
Sky . . . earth . . . stem . . . root
Leaf . . . green . . . sap
Soil . . . air
Seed
Soil . . . visible
Hidden . . . breathing . . . sucking
Bud . . . ooze . . . sun . . . damp
Light . . . dark . . . bright . . . decay . . . laugh
Tear . . . vein . . . rain . . . mud . . . branch . . . root

The wood carvings await
Within each uncut branch
The carver's knife

III - 8

Fourfold Representation Of The Mystery

B efore Heaven and Earth
There was something nebulous
Tranquil . . . effortless
Permeating universally
Revolving soundlessly
Fusing

It may be regarded as the Mother
Of all organic forms

Its name is not known nor its language
But it is called Tao

The ancient sages called it "great"
The Great Tao

Great means in harmony
In harmony means tuned in
Tuned in means going far
Going far means returning
To the harmony

The Tao is great
The coil of life is great
The body is great
The human is designed to be great

There are in existence four great notes
The human is made to be one thereof

When you place yourself in harmony with your body
The body tunes itself to the slow unfolding of life
Life flows in harmony with the Tao

All proceeds
Naturally
In tune

III - 9

The Seed Light

The seed light shines everywhere
All forms derive life from it

When bodies are created
It does not take possession

It clothes and feeds the ten thousand things
And does not disturb their illusions

Magical helix . . . smallest form
Mother of all forms

The living are born, flourish and disappear
Without knowing their seed creator
Helix of light

In all nature it is true that the wiser
The older and the greater
Reside in the smaller

III - 10

This Is It

The seed moves so slowly and serenely
Moment to moment
That it appears inactive

The garden at sunrise breathing
The quiet breath of twilight
Moment to moment to moment

When we are in tune with this blissful rhythm
The ten thousand forms flourish
Without effort

It is all so simple
Each next moment . . .
This is it!

III - 11

GATE OF THE SOFT MYSTERY

Valley of life
   Gate of the Soft Mystery
Beginnings in the lowest place
Gate of the Soft Mystery
Gate of the Dark Woman
Gate of the Soft Mystery
Seed of all living
Gate of the Soft Mystery
Constantly enduring
Gate of the Soft Mystery
Enter
Gently . . .

III - 12

The Lesson Of Seed

The soft overcomes the hard
The small overcomes the large
The gentle survives the strong
The invisible survives the visible

Fish should be left in deep water
Fire and iron kept under ground
Seed should be left free
To grow in the rhythm of life

PART IV

THE EXPERIENCE OF NEURAL ENERGY

HOMAGE TO THE EXTERNAL SENSES

IV - 1

SEEİПG

Open naked eye
Light . . . radiant . . . pulsating . . .
"I've been blind all my life to this radiance"

Retinal mandala
Swamp mosaic of rods and cones
Light rays hurtle into retina 186,000 miles per second
Cross scope
Retinal scripture

The Blind I
Recoils at glittering energy
Impersonal, mocking
Illusions of control
"Too bright! Turn it off!
Bring back the shadow world"

The Seer Eye
Vibrates to the trembling web of light
Merges with the seen
Merges with the scene
Slides down optical whirlpool
Through central needle point

IV - 2

HEARIПG

S ound waves, sound waves
Uncover lotus membrane
Trembling tattoo of
Sympathetic vibrations
Float along liquid canals

Single piano note
Meteor of delight
Collides with quivering membrane

Eternal note
Spins slowly
On vibrating thread

Ear you are
Sound waves

IV - 3

Touching

Extend your free
Nerve endings
Fine woven tendrils

Feel my fingers'
Soft landing on your creviced surface
Send sense balloon drifting up
Through miles of skin web
Tissue atmosphere of
Electric thrill contact

Soar free through epidermal space on
Shuddering fibres of breathless pleasure

IV - 4

Smelling

In the sensory landscape
Of tangled odors
Streaming belts of perfume
 Ecstatic breath
 Musk of glands
 Sexual allure
 Heaven scent
 Elixir of life

IV - 5

Tasting

The thin sheath
   Covering the tongue
Melts . . .

Exploding taste buds
Quivering tissue . . .
Mouth flowers

PART V

THE EXPERIENCE OF THE CHAKRAS

HOMAGE TO THE INTERNAL SENSES

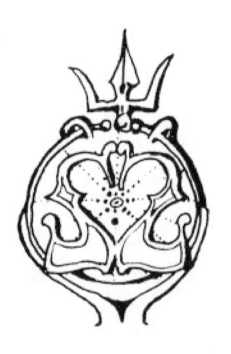

V - 1

THE ROOT CHAKRA

C an you float through the universe of your body
     and not lose your way?
Can you dissolve softly?
  Decompose?
Can you rest
  dormant seed-light
  buried in moist earth?
Can you drift
  single-celled
  in soft tissue swamp?
Can you sink
  into your dark
  fertile marsh?
Can you spiral slowly
  down the great central river?

V - 2

THE SEX CHAKRA

C an you float through the universe of your body
   and not lose your way?
Can you lie quietly
  engulfed
  in the slippery union
  of male and female?
  Warm wet dance of generation
  Endless ecstacies of lovers?
Can you offer your stamen trembling in the meadow
  for the electric penetration of pollen
  writhe together on the river bank
  coil serpentine
  while birds sing?
Become two cells merging?
Slide together in molecular embrace?
Can you, murmuring
Lose all . . .
Fusing

V - 3

THE HEART CHAKRA

Can you float through the universe of your body
　　and not lose your way?
Flow with fire-blood
Through each tissued corridor?

Can you let your heart
　pump down red tunnels
　stream into cell chambers?

Can you center on this
Heart-fire of love?

Can you let your heart
　pulse for all love
　beat for all sorrow
　throb for all pain
　thud for all joy
　swell for all mankind?

Can you let it flow
With compassion
For all life?

V - 4

THE THROAT CHAKRA

C an you float through the universe of your body
   and not lose your way?
Breathing
Can you drift into free air?
Rise on the trembling vibration
   of inhale and exhale?

Can you ascend the fragile thread of breath
   into cloud-blue bliss?
Can you spiral up through soft atmosphere
Breathing
Catch the moment between in-breath and out-breath
Just there . . .

Can you float beyond life and death
Breathing

V - 5

The Crown Chakra

Can you float through the universe of your body
        and not lose your way ?
Can you focus on the billion-celled diamond network
Pull the sensory streams into your brain
Create an incandescent solar flare
A thousand-petalled
Lotus of light?

V - 6

Ascending Ladder
Of Chakras

Drift along your body's soft swampland
   where warm mud sucks lazily

Feel each cell in your body communicating
   in serpent-coiled rainbow orgasm

Feel the sensuous rhythm of time
   pulsing life along the arterial network

Bring the ethereal breath of life into
   the white rooms of your brain

Radiate golden light out to
   the four corners of creation

PART VI

RE-ENTRY TO THE

IMPRINTED WORLD

HOMAGE TO THE SYMBOLIC MIND

VI - 1

THE MOMENT OF FULLNESS

Grab hold tightly
Let go lightly

The full cup can take no more
The candle burns down
The taut bow must be loosed
The razor edge cannot long endure

Nor this moment re-lived

So now . . .
Grab hold tightly
Now . . .
Let go lightly

VI - 2

How To Escape The Trap
Of Beauty And Goodness

As you return
Remember

Choose beauty, so you define ugly
Select good, so you create evil
As you choose your joy, so you design your sorrow

The coin you are now imprinting has two sides

Better to return in the flow of the Tao

For indeed
The opposites exist for you alone
Beyond your heads and tails
Dances the unity

All sounds harmonize
All games end in a tie

Your God stands on the pitcher's mound
    nods to his catcher
    winds up and throws
    a shoulder-high fast ball

Right into your Devil's glove

VI - 3

FOR GOD'S SAKE
—FEEL GOOD

As you return
Remember to choose consciously

Power is the heavy stone wrenched
  from your garden of tenderness

Virtue is the heavy stone
  crushing your innocence

What can be learned
From nature is
Harmony

Therefore
  Shun the social
  Cuddle the elemental
  Avoid angles, lie with the round
  Shun plastic, conspire with seed

Do no good
But for God's sake
Feel good
And Nature's order will prevail

VI - 4

Re-Imprinting
With Water As Element

R emember
 The flow of water

Live at the natural level
fluid

Live close to earth
fluid

Live giving life
fluid

Live falling free
fluid

Live in the stream
fluid

VI - 5

THE LESSON OF WATER

What one values in the game
   is the play

What one values in the form
   is the moment of forming

What one values in the house
   is the moment of dwelling

What one values in the heart
   is the beating

What one values in the action
   is the timing

Indeed
Because you flow like water
You can neither win nor lose

VI - 6

ᵀHE UᵗiLiᵗY OF ᴨoᵗHiᴨG

The Nothing at the center of the thirty-spoke wheel . . .

The Nothing of the clay vase . . .

The Nothing within the four walls . . .

The goal of the game is to go beyond the game

You lose your mind

To use your head

You lose your mind

To use your head

VI - 7

The Innosense Of The Sensual

Name the five colors–
shadow the eye

Name the eight notes–
muffle the ear

Name the five tastes–
coat the tongue

Naming stops the flow

Win the game, lose the play

Let innosense
Direct your desire

VI - 8

What The Brain Said To The Mind

One to me is fame and shame
One to me is loss and gain
One to me is pleasure and pain
Murmured the brain

Looking down with compassionate curiosity
As a beautiful woman idly
Inspects a tiny blemish
On her long smooth flank

Looking down with compassionate curiosity
At the small imprinted
Chess board
Of the mind's external game

One to me is shame and fame . . .

VI - 9

How To Recognize The Tao Imprint

One who returns in the flow of Tao
  Brings back a mysterious penetration
So subtle
That it is misunderstood

Hesitant like one who wades in
  a stream at winter
Wary as a man in ambush
Considerate as a welcome guest
Fluid like a mountain stream
Natural as uncarved wood
Floating high like a gull
Unfathomable like muddy water

How can we fathom this muddiness?
Water becomes clear through stillness

How can we become still?
By moving with the stream

VI - 10

ILLUSTRATION OF
A TAO IMPRINT

He stands apart
        serene
curiously observing

He stands quietly
looking forlorn
like an infant who has not yet
learned to know what to smile at

He is a little sad for what he sees

While others enjoy their possessions
he lazily drifts, a homeless
do-nothing, owning nothing

Or he moves slowly close to the land

While others are crisp and definite
he seems indecisive

He does not appear to be making his way
in the world

He is different

A wise infant nursing at the breast
Of all life Inside

VI - 11

KEEP IN TOUCH

The Tao flows everywhere

Keep in touch
Be at home
Everywhere

He who loses the contact
Is alone
Everywhere

Keeping in touch with the Tao
Is called
Harmony

VI - 12

USE YOUR KNOWLEDGE
OF NATURE'S LAW

Nature's way is to leave no residue
All is absorbed

Therefore we treasure the "least of men"

All belongs
All is salvaged
Nothing is rejected

This is called Stealing the Light . . .
Nature's subtle secret

VI - 13

The Conscious Application Of Strength

Force recoils
But
The time comes
When there is nothing to do
Except act consciously
With courage

VI - 14

Victory Celebration

C elebrate your victory
with funeral rites
for your slain illusions

Wear some black at your wedding

VI - 15

ALONG THE GRAIN

The Tao is nameless
Like uncarved wood

As soon as it is carved
There are names

Carve carefully
Along the grain

VI - 16

He Who Knows
The Center Endures

Who knows the outside is clever
Who knows the center endures
Who masters others gains robot power
Who comes to the center has flowering strength

Faith of consciousness is freedom
Hope of consciousness is strength
Love of consciousness evokes the same in return

Faith of seed frees
Hope of seed flowers
Love of seed grows

VI - 17

WALK CAREFULLY
WHEN YOU ARE AMONG . . .

Holy men and
Righteous deeds
Distract from the internal

Learned men
Distract from natural wisdom

Professional know-how
Addicts people to the contrived and external

Be respectful and compassionate
But walk carefully when you are among—

> learned men and doctors
> holy men
> government officials
> publishers
> professors
> religious leaders
> psychologists and social scientists
> women with beautiful faces
> artists and writers
> people who charge fees
> city men and rich people

movie makers and reporters
people who want to help you
people who want help
Christians and Jews
For such as these, however well meaning
Place you on their chessboard
Addict you to their externals
Distract you from
The Tao within

The lesson of the Tao is more likely
to be found among—
gardener, hermits and eccentrics
people who build their own homes
children and parents who learn from them
amateur musicians and wanderers
serene psychotics
animals
those who look at sunsetsand walk in the woods
beautiful women
cooks and bakers of bread
people who sit by the fire
couples who have been in love for years
smiling men with bad reputations

PART VII

POEMS ON
THE CONDUCT OF LIFE

WITH ROSEMARY WOODRUFF LEARY

(1969)

VII-1

CONCERNING DOSAGE
AND CAPACITY

When
I am
Of highest capacity
It flows through me

When
I am
Of middling capacity
I write poems about the flowing

When
I am
Of low capacity
The flow irritates me

VII-2

THE PERFECT PARADOX

The perfect
Contains
The imperfect

The great design
Contains
Deliberate flaw

Error
Is the architect
Of evolution

The complete life
An infinite series
Of timely accidents

Each blundering moment
A perfect part
Of the perfected hole

Attention Readers: *If you can detect the three mistakes in this poem you will win a black and white pony*

VII-3

Terra Story

From ancient times
It has been known that
A man and woman
Are as rich
As the broad land
Through which
They wander freely

Sitting here
In front of our flimsy
Mountain cottage
We see
No wall
No buildings
No neighbors

VII-4

Ͱhis Desigɴ Has ɴo Plaɴ

Ͱhere is no pure white
   The Tao forever blending
There is no perfect human
   The Tao forever bending
Great space has no corners
   The Tao never ending
Great music is faintly heard
   The Tao forever sending
This design has no plan
   It's forever mending

mending patching up giraffes making do mutants false
starts bulging-eyed frogs goofs some catastrophic misfits
smog The Timing's Off! Emergency Stopgap Measures
Adapt Survive For God's Sake Don't Ask Me Why!
Malthusian fuckups Darwinian losers not another Ice Age
humus top soil shit There Goes My Paleolithic Garden!

Listen sisters and brothers
There's no shortage of anything . . .
   The Tao forever mending
   The Tao profusely lending
   Blending . . . bending . . . sending
   Forever ending
   Never ending

VII-5

What Now?

Out of Tao
The One
Is born

Out of the One
The Two
Divide

Out of the Two mated
We created
The Three

It's fun to blend
But where will it end
And what will become
Of our coming?

Consider the mathematics
Clicked the DNA computer
Softly

One = done
Two = nothing new
Three = variety

When multiplied
10,000 forms are supplied
With fins, feathers
and all sorts of furry coverings
What is the name
Of this inexhaustibly inventive game?

We inquired as we
Lay in each others' arms.

Will it grow tired
Will it grow tame
As we excel
In playing this game
Always cooped up
In a permeable cell?

Is it time to re-enter
The center?

What now
Great Tao?

PART VIII

HOMAGE TO THE AWE-FULL SEER

(1967)

Leary in Millbrook, 1966.

VIII-1

HOMAGE TO
THE AWE-FULL SEER

At each beat
in the Earth's rotating dance
there is born "   "
a momentary cluster of molecules
possessing the transient ability to know-see-experience
its own place in the evolutionary spiral.

Such an organism, such an event
senses exactly where he or she is
in the billion-year-old ballet.

They are able to trace back
the history of the deoxyribonucleic thread
of which they are both conductive element and
      current.
They can experience the next moment
in its million to the millionth meaning.
Exactly that.

Some divine seers are recognized for this unique
      capacity.
Those that are recognized
are called and killed by various names.
Most of them are not recognized—

they float through life
like a snowflake
kissing the earth.
No one ever hears them murmur
"Ah there"
At the moment of impact.

Seers are aware of each other's existence
the way each particle in the hurtling nuclear trapeze
is aware of other particles.
They move too fast to give names
to themselves or each other.

Such people can be described in terms
no more precise or less foolish
than the descriptive equations of nuclear physics.
They have no more or less meaning
in the cultural games of life
than electrons have in the game of chess.
They are present but cannot be perceived or
          categorized.
They exist at a level beyond
the black and white squares of the game board.
The function of "   " is to teach.

Take an apple and slice it down the middle.
A thin red circle surrounds
          the gleaming white meat.

In the center is a dark seed
whose function is beyond any of your games.
If you knew how to listen
the seed would hum you a seed-song.

The divine incarnates teach
like a snowflake caught in the hand teaches.
Once you speak the message you have lost it.
Once you know the message you no longer have it.
The seed becomes a dried pit, the snowflake
a film of water on your hand.

Wise seers are continually
exploding in beautiful dance.
Like a speckled fish
dying in your hand
as its eye looks at you unblinking.
Like the virus fragmenting
divine beauty in the grasp of tissue.

Now and then the "   " sings
words beyond rational comprehension.
The message is always the same
though the sounds, the scratched rhumba
of inkmarks is always different.

It's like Einstein's equation felt as orgasm.
The serpent unwinds up the spine,
mushrooms like a lotus sunflare in the skull.
If I tell you that the apple seed message
hums the drone of a Hindu flute
will that stop the drone?

The secret of "   " must always be secret.
Divine sage recognized, message lost.
Snowflake caught, pattern changed.
They dance out the pattern without being
        recognized.
Caught in the act, they melt in your hand.

The message then contained in a drop of water
involves another chase for the infinite.
The sign of "   " is change and anonymity.
As soon as you try to glorify
sanctify, worship, deify the seer
you have killed him.

Thus the Pharisees
performed a merry, holy ballet.
All praise to them!
It is the Christians who kill Christ.

As soon as you invent a symbol
give "   " a name
you assassinate the process
to serve your own ends.
To speak the name of Buddha
Christ
Lao Tse—
except as a sudden ecstatic breath—
is to murder the living God
fix him with your preservative
razor him onto a microscope slide
sell him for profit in your biological supply house.

The seers have no function
but they produce in others the ecstatic gasp
the uncontrollable visionary laugh.
Too much!
So what!
Why not!
The stark stare of wonder.
Awful!
Awe-full!

He who knows

nothing of red fire
win be red water
love of red green
in the red flowers

IN TAO WE TRUST

Notes

PART I

I - 1   Adapted from Tao Chapter 17. Elsewhere titled: "Rulers" in *The Wisdom of Lao Tse,* edited by Lin Yutang, Modern Library, New York, 1948; "The Unadulterated Influence" in *The Texts of Taoism,* translated by James Legge, Dover, New York, 1962. (Hereafter, the initials LYT designate Lin Yutang and the initials JL designate James Legge.)

I - 2   Adapted from Tao Chapter 18. Elsewhere titled: "The Decline of Tao," LYT; "The Decay of Manners," JL.

I - 3   Adapted from Tao Chapter 35. Elsewhere titled: "The Peace of Tao," LYT; "The Attribute of Benevolence," JL.

I - 4   Adapted from Tao Chapter 19. Elsewhere titled: "Realize the Simple Self," LYT; "Returning to the Unadulerated Influence," JL.

I - 5   Adapted from Tao Chapter 23. Elsewhere titled: "The Dregs and Tumors of Virtue," LYT; "Painful Graciousness," JL.

PART II

II - 1   Adapted from Tao Chapter 1. Elsewhere titled: "On the Absolute Tao," LYT; "Embodying the Tao," JL.

II - 2   Adapted from Tao Chapter 4. Elsewhere titled: "The Character of Tao," LYT; "The Fountainless,"JL.

II - 3   Adapted from Tao Chapter 5. Elsewhere titled: "Nature," LYT; "The Use of Emptiness," JL.

II - 4   Adapted from Tao Chapter 26. Elsewhere titled: "Heaviness and Lightness," LYT; "The Quality of Gravity," JL.

II - 5   Adapted from Tao Chapter 7. Elsewhere titled: "Living for Others," LYT; "Sheathing the Light," JL.

II - 6   Adapted from Tao Chapter 14. Elsewhere titled: "Prehistoric Origins," LYT; "The Manifestation of the Mystery," JL.

II - 7   Adapted from Tao Chapter 29. Elsewhere titled: "Warning Against Interference," LYT; "Taking No Action," JL.

II-8   Adapted from Tao Chapter 5. Elsewhere titled: "Nature," LYT; "The Use of Emptiness," JL.

II-9   Adapted from Tao Chapter 36. Elsewhere titled: "The Rhythm of Life," LYT; "Minimizing the Light," JL.

PART III

III - 1   Adapted from Tao Chapter 14. Elsewhere titled: "Prehistoric Origins," LYT; "The Manifestation of the Mystery," JL.

III - 2   Adapted from Tao Chapter 14. Elsewhere titled: "Prehistoric Origins," LYT; "The Manifestation of the Mystery," JL.

III - 3   Adapted from Tao Chapter 15. Elsewhere titled: "The Wise Ones of Old," LYT; "The Exhibition of the Qualities of the Tao," JL.

III - 4   Adapted from Tao Chapter 16. Elsewhere titled: "Knowing the Eternal Law," LYT; "Returning to the Root," JL.

III - 5   Adapted from Tao Chapter 21. Elsewhere titled: "Manifestations of Tao," LYT; "The Empty Heart, or the Tao In its Operation," JL.

III - 6   Adapted from Tao Chapter 22. Elsewhere titled: "Futility of Contention," LYT; "Returning to Simplicity," JL.

III - 7   Adapted from Tao Chapter 28. Elsewhere titled: "Keeping to the Female," LYT; "Returning to Simplicity," JL.

III - 8   Adapted from Tao Chapter 25. Elsewhere titled: "The Four Eternal Models," LYT; "Representations of the Mystery," JL.

III - 9   Adapted from Tao Chapter 34. Elsewhere titled: "The Great Tao
           Flows Everywhere," LYT; "The Task of Achievement," JL.

III-10   Adapted from Tao Chapter 37. Elsewhere titled: "World Peace,"
           LYT; "The Exercise of Government," JL.

III-11   Adapted from Tao Chapter 6. Elsewhere titled: "The Spirit of the
           Valley," LYT; "The Completion of Material Forms," JL.

III-12   Adapted from Tao Chapter 36. Elsewhere titled: "The Rhythm of
           Life," LYT; "Minimizing the Light," JL.

PART IV

IV 1-5   Adapted from Tao Chapter 12. Elsewhere titled: "The Senses,"
           LYT; "The Repression of the Desires," JL.

PART V

V 1-6   Adapted from Tao Chapter 10. Elsewhere titled: "Embracing the
           One," LYT; "Possibilities Through the Tao," JL.

PART VI

VI - 1   Adapted from Tao Chapter 9. Elsewhere titled: "The Danger of
           Overweening Success," LYT; "Fullness and Complacency Contrary
           to the Tao," JL.

VI - 2   Adapted from Tao Chapter 2. Elsewhere titled: "The Rise of Relative
           Opposites," LYT; "The Nourishment of the Person," JL.

VI - 3   Adapted from Tao Chapter 3. Elsewhere titled: "Action Without
           Deeds," LYT; "Keeping the People at Rest," JL.

VI - 4   Adapted from Tao Chapter 8. Elsewhere titled: "Water," LYT; "The
           Placid and Contented Nature," JL.

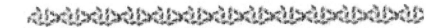

VI - 5   Adapted from Tao Chapter 8. Elsewhere titled: "Water," LYT; "The Placid and Contented Nature," JL.

VI - 6   Adapted from Tao Chapter 1. Elsewhere titled: "The Utility of Not-being," LYT; "The Use of What Has No Substantive Existence," JL.

VI - 7   Adapted from Tao Chapter 12. Elsewhere titled: "The Senses," LYT; "The Repression of the Desires," JL.

VI - 8   Adapted from Tao Chapter 13. Elsewhere titled: "Praise and Blame," LYT; "Loathing Shame," JL.

VI - 9   Adapted from Tao Chapter 15. Elsewhere titled: "The Wise Ones of Old," LYT; "The Exhibition of the Qualities of the Tao," JL.

VI-10   Adapted from Tao Chapter 20. Elsewhere titled: "The World and I," LYT; "Being Different from Ordinary Men," JL.

VI-11   Adapted from Tao Chapter 23. Elsewhere titled: "Identification with Tao," LYT; "Absolute Vacancy," JL.

VI-12   Adapted from Tao Chapter 27. Elsewhere titled: "On Stealing the Light," LYT; "Dexterity in Using Tao," JL.

VI-13   Adapted from Tao Chapter 30. Elsewhere titled "Warning Against the Use of Force," LYT; "A Caveat Against War," JL.

VI-14   Adapted from Tao Chapter 31. Elsewhere titled: "Weapons of Evil," LYT; "Stilling War," JL.

VI-15   Adapted from Tao Chapter 32. Elsewhere titled: "Tao Is Like the Sea," LYT; "The Tao With No Name," JL.

VI-16   Adapted from Tao chapter 33. Elsewhere titled: "Knowing Oneself," LYT; "Discriminating Between Attributes," JL.

VI-17   Adapted from Tao Chapter 19. Elsewhere titled: "Realize the Simple Self," LYT; "Returning to the Unadulterated Influence," JL.

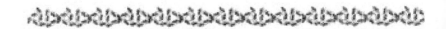

PART V11

1-5   Adapted from Tao Chapters 41-45.

PART VIII

A tribute to Lao Tse.

Chinese ideograms for
Tao Te Ching.

Index

ACCORDING TO THE ORDER OF THE TAO TE CHING

RECORD YOUR POEMS
HERE

Ronin Books for Independent Minds